AMERICA'S PERIGON

AMERICA'S PERIGON

BOBBY JEFFRIES
Roger Stone

RJJ, LLC.

America's Perigon
Bobby Jeffries

Published by RJJ, LLC
First published September 2020

"The problems of the world cannot possibly be solved by skeptics or cynics whose horizons are limited by the obvious realities. We need men who can dream of things that never were and ask why not?"

—*JOHN F. KENNEDY*

CONTENTS

FOREWARD

A s someone who has advised several Presidential candidates, three Presidents and many political leaders while being a participant in eleven Presidential races, I view the connection between Lincoln, Kennedy, Reagan and Trump as a multi-generational continuation of American Greatness. Robert "Bobby" Jeffries does a great job of analyzing the traits, traditions and beliefs that bind these leaders together.

Their adherence to the ideals of liberty and freedom was resolute and never wavered. Each was committed to democracy, free-enterprise, capitalism and Constitutional liberty.

At the same time we must understand the pivotal role of Presidents Truman, Eisenhower and Nixon in the bi-partisan commitment to freedom and bi-partisan opposition to Communism that framed that continuum and defined both parties until 2020 when one of our major parties abandoned both democracy and capitalism for the false promise of socialism.

America's Perigon explores these connections and tells us why we must look towards the past to move forward into this new era. Sadly, the current political climate does not allow for intellectual or in-depth explorations of our past and where we need to go in the future. America has plunged into a deeply divided realm where we are constantly divided and pitted against one another to the benefit of the powerful elite.

Rather than follow the tradition of generously conceding defeat and working with a new President to help the country, the power elite have launched at least three coup attempts to topple the President. This would have ended the political tradition that binds our greatest Presidents together.

In order for our nation to move forward towards our destiny, we must recognize the strengths of our founding documents and the people that have driven our success since we gained our independence. With the rampant censorship and political persecutions going on across America, the exchange of these ideals is more crucial now than ever. We cannot let them deny us our hero's.

This is no longer about being a Republican or Democrat, it is about the American way. This is about the elite insiders for whom there are no rules and no law versus those like Kennedy, Reagan and Trump who were outsiders and reformers opposed by the elite. Our success and greatness is not determined by our political affiliations, it's about whether or not we stand on the side of freedom or tyranny.

Restoring America and protecting ourselves against the dangerous ideas of globalism and groupthink will not be easy. However, we must not be silent, and we cannot stop innovating and pushing for a return to re-examining and implanting the ideals that created the most free and liber-ated nation to ever exist.

Bobby Jeffries is someone I know has the energy, vigor and tenacity to put these words on paper. Do you have the courage and drive to demand a return to a nation that our Founding Fathers would be proud of?

-Roger Stone
Florida
July 21, 2020

Photo provided by Roger Stone

Photo provided by Roger Stone

PREFACE

Fellow citizens, like so many of you, I too come from an ordinary, hard-working, middle-class, all American family. And yes, I voted for President Donald J. Trump in 2016, though it was not because he was running on the GOP ticket. I voted for him because I trusted the wisdom and judgment of a gentleman I loved and deeply respected. That man was my late grandfather, a giant of a man, a giant of an American, and my greatest hero.

My grandfather was a member of America's greatest generation. When he grew up, all of our nation's most timeless values and sacred principles were alive, well, and ever-present for all Americans. Thus, one's pursuit of the American Dream was very much attainable for all those who chose to put in the effort to pursue the promise of a better future. Like many others of that heroic generation, he was a big believer in the American Dream.

He worked hard to become living proof of it. First, as a young man running his family farm, to serving his beloved country in the United States Army, then finally achieving great success in the world of business. Of course, his most enormous pride and joy came from the vibrant family he and my grandmother built together, and they did it the American way.

For my grandparents, and likely yours if you are a millennial, there was nothing more important than preserving the American Dream. That promise ensured their right to worship and protected the God-given freedoms and civil liberties our founders guaranteed to us all in the Constitution. Similar to our founders, he and my grandmother were never too crazy about the political parties themselves.

Regarding politics, both supported only the finest and proudest patriots. They had to display the courage to conserve our freedom as well as our sacred American establishing principles.

Thus, both were ardent supporters of John F. Kennedy and his New Frontier in the 60s, and in the 80s, Ronald Reagan and his Bright New Dawn for America. They loved these two pillars of modern American history because they embodied America's timeless and revolutionary spirit. That is what they instilled in their children and grandchildren to serve as the standard by which to hold our leaders.

Unfortunately, my grandfather got very sick after my grandmother passed away. Before going home to the Lord and his beloved wife, he would articulate his and our families' sacred principles to carry on to my children one day.

Each time I visited him, we would talk about life, about America, and watch television together on a miniature tv monitor attached to the hospital bed. Typically, we would only watch three programs, Law and Order, cable news, and his favorite, Donald Trump's hit show, "The Apprentice."

My grandfather was old school, he was a man's man, and he

was tough. He admired brutal honesty, integrity, and balls (courage) not only to do the right thing but always tell the truth even when it hurts.

Therefore, you can probably imagine he was intrigued and impressed by Donald Trump's strong and confident demeanor on that highly successful reality television show. It struck him so much that he would often say that America needed a businessman in the White House to fix our broken and deeply corrupt political system.

Fast forward to 2015, and Donald Trump finally announced his candidacy for the president of the United States. While many Americans had doubts about Trump, I didn't, for I knew my grandfather would be fully on board with Trump's mission to fix our broken country.

In my heart, I know he and my grandmother watch every one of Trump's rally's cheering U-S-A, U-S-A, U-S-A amongst the loudest of God's most beautiful angels in heaven. I dedicate this book to them and, of course, my beloved mother who stood at my side the very day where I first witnessed the return of America's spirit with my own two eyes, in Middletown PA, at a Trump rally in November of 2017.

**Discussing tax reform with Sean Hannity in
Middletown PA, November 2017**
Photo provided by Sally Walborn

I also dedicate this book to Roger Stone, my friend, mentor, and the first person in politics to believe in me and my brand. The idea for this book came to me while sitting in the passenger seat of his Jaguar on the way to the airport after a long afternoon of cigars and lively political discussion.

At the Stone Zone, 2017
Photo provided by the Author

Over the past few years, I have had the honor and privilege of his careful guidance. The knowledge I have obtained from him has been immeasurable. Most of all, he has taught me the importance of loyalty, to one's friends, one's country, and one's values. Roger demonstrated that same brand of loyalty to his nation, his God, and his dear friend of forty years, President Donald J. Trump in a two year politically motivated witch hunt. Despite all the pressure, Roger refused to bear false witness against our president. It was my profound honor to be there in the DC courtroom to support him and the Stone family.

I also dedicate this book to my good friend Jacob Engels, who the Daily Beast once described as Roger Stone's "Mini-Me", and for a good reason. Having learned at the knee of Stone himself, Jacob is not only one of America's most hard-hitting investigative journalists, but one of her most brilliant political minds. Undoubtedly, he has already proven himself to be the "Roger Stone" of our generation.

Finally, I must dedicate this book to all the patriots for whom I have shared some of my life's fondest memories while traveling this beautiful country. It was on the front lines of freedom where each of us first bore witness to America's Perigon together. Without those special people and those life-changing experiences, this book would never have been possible.

-Bobby Jeffries
Hershey, Pennsylvania
August 11, 2020

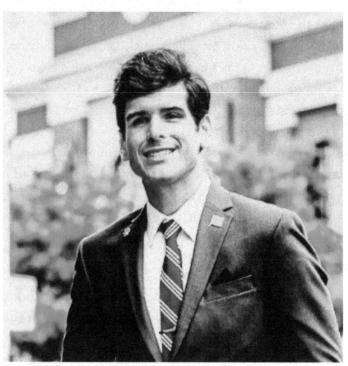
Photo provided by the Author

CHAPTER 1

Oh, Say Can You See?

"THE TRUTH IS THE LIGHT AND THE LIGHT IS THE TRUTH."

- RALPH ELLISON

In this new decade of the 20s, the American people stand at the most significant turning point in the history of our nation. Collectively, each of us as Americans of every generation faces the most rigorous and gravest decisions of all time, as we crossover from one side of this familiar corridor of history into a brave new era.

This narrow hallway is dark and ever abundant with uncertainty and challenge, that much is clear. But so is the light at the end of the tunnel peering through for all to see, if only we have the nerve and vision to see it. That light is as bright as the rays of a thousand suns, and it is shining brightly upon a better future for the United States and her people. It is a guide we must use to proceed onward.

At the end of this tunnel, a dawn of infinite potential awaits all Americans, where new progress, continued advancement, and complete technology everywhere around us will not only be our forefront but provide us with the necessary inertia to carry this nation toward fulfilling our innate historical purpose and destiny. That destiny belongs to every American citizen, equally.

For us to fulfill it, we must summon the courage and confidence within ourselves not only to endure but to believe in ourselves and our dreams once again. After all, this is America, the ultimate land of opportunity where everything and anything worthwhile is achievable for those willing to work hard and believe. For without the expectation of hope and prosperity intact, we will lose sight of that promising horizon.

Trusting ourselves, and in the well of unlimited potential at our fingertips as citizens of this great nation, are essential. We already have all we will ever need to will our innate American dreams into reality.

Those of us who recognize this truth find it very difficult to witness our fellow citizens today who turn a blind eye to it. Watching their willingness to yield powerful tools like freedom, individual liberty, and free thought is undoubtedly painful, because those tools are what is required to make our dreams a reality.

The vast number of human beings throughout history and those around the world today, merely existing, not living, under tyrannical and oppressive governments, would not only agree, but do just about anything to possess the blessings for which we have here in the United States.

Our founders that broke away from the tyranny described would agree.

Additionally, to them, it would be utter lunacy for those Americans today who are willing to give up the freedoms and civil liberties for which they dedicated their lives attaining. Such acts not only signal grave miscalculation but a betrayal of the highest order to this nation as well as to themselves.

On the other hand, they would see that these challenging times have crippled many Americans into submission. They find themselves in a dark place of utter fear, anxiety, and Stockholm syndrome at which they could not possibly discern the light of truth nor the big picture.

Like those American colonists among them who did not see the big picture then, we must continue to endure and show them the light of truth as they did. Because they too matter. The hopes, dreams, and ideas within the minds of all of us are the very seeds and building blocks to any future, let alone a future worthy of America's unlimited potential.

Why is that potential there in the first place? Because our founding fathers had to endure through their own dark and narrow corridor of history, with only a flicker of light as their guide. But in their great wisdom, they knew that light was worth following.

At the end of their tunnel was the freedom and independence to which they dedicated their lives to attain. A brand-new nation founded upon the same timeless and indispensable principles needed to move America and her people forward. To our founders, greatness was inevitable if only we fought hard to keep those principals intact.

How did they achieve this?

With their spirit, which was innately American, forged from the courage of that generation and rising to the occasion with equal vigor. It was more than enough for them to empower the young patriots at their command. They harnessed its limitless fuel not only to endure but also to propel them through the darkness to the light of a better future.

That unstoppable spirit established something the world had never seen or fathomed possible. A shiny city upon a hill, the United States of America, the last bastion of freedom on earth, built on a foundation of sacred principles required for any lasting and durable society to reach its potential.

To this day, those sacred principles, combined with their vigorous American spirit, is still the most potent and effective recipe on earth for infinite strength and creation. Therefore, the most important choice we have to make as Americans is to accept our responsibility to ourselves, our nation, and our future, and defend their survival.

Although the revolution to which our founders fought ended in victory, every great leader throughout our history understands, as they did, that the victory was only temporary. The ongoing struggle to defend and maintain our freedoms was not over then, now, or ever.

CHAPTER 2

Heirs of that First Revolution

"WE DARE NOT FORGET THAT WE ARE THE HEIRS OF THAT FIRST REVOLUTION."

- JOHN F. KENNEDY

A wise man once said that we, the American people, are the heirs of that first revolution, and he was right. However, as its heirs, every generation of Americans must understand why our founders fought that war in the first place as well as accept the certainty that the spoils of that epic victory are not assured.

Yes, our American Revolution is the greatest underdog success story ever told. It occurred because our founders wanted to live their lives on their terms and not those of a tyrannical empire located across the ocean.

Despite being outmanned and facing overwhelming odds, our founders persevered. They did so because they were tired of the status quo, which produced unnecessary burdens, taxes, and a lack of options and opportunities they knew were deserved by any sovereign people.

Thus, these patriots bet on themselves and their home, cutting all roads behind them, and achieved an improbable victory through a superior understanding and innate awareness of their home terrain combined with their unbreakable American spirit.

In their brilliance, they knew, however, that their victory was only a temporary one, and the struggle and responsibility to preserve their newfound independence and freedom would not only be ongoing, but would fall on every generation of Americans after them to protect and maintain.

Founding father Benjamin Franklin, for example, was asked by a woman after the constitutional convention if the new form of government was to be a monarchy or a republic.

Franklin replied: "A republic, if you can keep it."

Unlike any other founding government document in history, our United States Constitution grants the American people the power to elect those who govern us and ensure our freedoms and civil liberties. Thus, the responsibility is on the American people to defend them by selecting leaders worthy enough to lead and represent us in government and stay true to our nation's founding principles and our founders' vision.

Our first president, George Washington, was the unquestioned leader among our founders, both during his time leading the continental army and time as president. Washington hated being referred to as a king, and thus instructed his peers to address him only as "Mr. President." After two terms, he left the office of the presidency after establishing a firm foundation for the new country.

Besides Washington, perhaps the greatest among our founders was Thomas Jefferson, the author of the Declaration of Independence, our first secretary of state, and ultimately our third president after John Adams. He was not only a genius but the epitome of patriotism, who established our first political party, the Democrat-Republican party, on our nation's core founding principles.

As president, he vastly expanded our country's territory, cementing the United States as a force for trade and commerce in the world, with the Louisiana Purchase substantially raising our prestige. While governing as president, Jefferson adhered to the founding documents for which he played such a critical role in drafting.

Undoubtedly, his great passion for and adherence to America's revolutionary principles laid a firm foundation of leadership, and like Washington, provided a legendary example to which future generations of Americans would study for guidance and inspiration.

However, following the departure of these great legends, America began to suffer without their guidance and great wisdom. By the mid-1800s, America was broken and divided, as were the political parties of that era.

Both Jefferson's Democratic-Republican party and the other major party of the day, the Whig party, were imploding at a fast rate due to obsolescence and systemic corruption. These twin challenges made it impossible for them to produce leaders with the courage to adhere to our nation's founding principles and use them as a guide to tackle the issues for which the founders left for future generations.

Thus, the American people desperately needed a leader who transcended partisan politics. Someone who possessed the innate courage to disrupt a broken and outdated status quo by voicing the uncomfortable truths for which the political establishment of the day did not want to hear, with brutal honesty, and unite our divided citizenry. Only a leader on par with our founders could bring the country and its politics full circle, back to our nation's founding principles, and combine those principles with solutions equal to the times.

By the grace of God, the American people were blessed with just such a leader in Abraham Lincoln.

"THOSE WHO DENY FREEDOM TO OTHERS, DESERVE IT NOT FOR THEMSELVES"

- ABRAHAM LINCOLN

'Honest' Abe Lincoln's understanding of his country and its destiny were not only on par with, but also comparable to that of our founding fathers. He was a great admirer of their timeless revolutionary spirit and the principles that birthed our nation. As he once said, "The principles of Jefferson are the definitions and the axioms of a free society." Therefore, Lincoln left the broken and dying Whig Party and founded a new party built on the same timeless principles of Jefferson and the founders.

The new Republican Party or GOP was indeed the grand old party of the republic, but it was superior to both parties of the era. Lincoln's new party took the founder's principles a step further by addressing and staunchly opposing the proverbial elephant in the room, the systemic cancer of slavery.

In his wisdom, Lincoln understood full well that he and his generation had the sacred duty, as the heirs of that first revolution, to not only protect and defend its spoils, but also take that revolution one step further with new solutions that equaled the times. Addressing this grave and moral issue that our founders' generation would not touch, not only fulfilled Lincoln's duty as the rightful heir of our American Revolution, but also expanded freedom even further for all Americans by abolishing slavery once and for all.

It was Lincoln's brutal honesty, innate courage, an intrinsic understanding of America's revolutionary spirit combined with his decisive leadership that won the Civil War, united a hopelessly divided citizenry, and ended the scourge of slavery.

Having the courage to disrupt the broken status quo and push back against injustice by voicing truths, no matter how hard it is for others to hear, is no easy task. Neither is fighting the good fight for the sake of advancing society and the human condition. Still, it is ultimately the right thing to do; however, doing so brings many enemies and critics, and Lincoln had plenty of both.

We all know what happened next, and America lost a legendary hero who would have undoubtedly accomplished even more had he been given a second term in office. However, Abraham Lincoln's legacy still lives on today and will forever because he was more than just a politician. He was more significant than politics itself, because like so few throughout our history, Lincoln was a champion for America and all of her people.

Moreover, he was precisely the leader for which the country so desperately needed to bring our country full circle and transform our broken political system to fit a new era, just as our founders did upon our nation's birth.

There will never be another Honest Abe Lincoln. His combination of courage, honesty, foresight, and wisdom are rare, and those capable of combining them to lead the American people forward are few and far between. Nevertheless, all these years later, we have observed our country and its politics come full circle.

CHAPTER 3

America's Perigon

"THE WHEEL IS COME FULL CIRCLE."
- WILLIAM SHAKESPEARE

The definition of a "Perigon" is something undergoing a complete 360-degree circle. Lincoln was precisely the leader for which America so desperately needed to bring its spirit and politics, full circle. This metamorphosis set the stage for the next chapter in American history. Therefore, he is undoubtedly the catalyst for America's very first Perigon. Unfortunately, many Americans still do not see this or the big picture.

Remember, all those like President Lincoln, who dare to disrupt the tired, broken status quo of the past, by speaking truth no matter how hard it is for some to hear, are always met with disdain and contempt. Today, no one on the face of the earth knows or has experienced this more than America's 45th President, Donald J. Trump. He is the catalyst for yet another display of our nation and its politics coming full circle.

Time and events allowed for another great disrupter's improbable rise to the presidency when America needed to regain its spirit to move forward, just as they did for Lincoln. Honest Abe utilized the best qualities of the great disrupters of his era as a template, whether we're talking about Thomas Jefferson's soaring idealism and revolutionary principles or the toughness and fighting spirit of Andrew Jackson. The fact is that the American people were longing for these traits again, and Lincoln coupled them masterfully with his honesty and charisma to be the peoples champion America required and deserved.

Everyone is a product of the time on which they grew, and Donald J. Trump is no different, for he too is using the two greatest disrupters and most significant political figures of the modern era, and combining their greatest strengths with his

own. Throughout this book, I will explain the correlation between John F. Kennedy and Ronald Reagan and how both
men led the American people with the same brand of all-
American leadership that guides Trump.

These two great leaders were not merely just storied Republicans and Democrats, they were champions of the American
people, whose brand of leadership operated above partisan
politics. That is why Democrats and Republicans alike have
been waiting and longing for the next Kennedy and the next
Reagan; it is also why members of both parties revere both
men.

In Trump, we have the best qualities of both presidents, the
idealism of John F. Kennedy, and the strong, principled leadership of Reagan combined with his very own brand of
straight talk. Under his watch, our courageous founders' gold
standard of leadership, which was refined and polished by
Lincoln, has come full circle along the seasonal path of history.

As we have long commemorated in the vast and ever-expand-
ing realm of cinema and film, we observe that reboots and remakes don't always capture the greatness of the original. Some
remakes do, others don't, and some blow the first right out
of the water. But what remains consistent is that they are all
inherently different. Still, timing is the ultimate decider of
success or failure, whether one refers to the success of a new
movie, or even a broken country in desperate need of a reality
check.

Fortunately, in our country's case, the timing could not have been more ideal for a great disrupter like Lincoln, who brought about the return of the American spirit, and with it, a wholly renewed and reinvigorated America.

Our country and its politics have come full circle as they did in the days of Lincoln. I am not referring to rewinding the clock to an obsolete America that is culturally exclusive, societally close-minded, nor one incapable of implementing new trailblazing solutions. Nor an America that settles for incompetent, self-serving leaders, ill-equipped and unmotivated to embrace, empower, and include all of its fellow citizens in the promise of everything our freedom has to offer.

No, I am referring to an America that has finally been able to put the proverbial plug back into the wall outlet, and turn a country that had been shut off for so long, back on once again. Hence, we transition back to the kind of greatness worthy of freedom's boundless potential, and to which we desperately need in this next decade. Remember, the defining purpose of Donald Trump's improbable rise to the presidency was to "Make America Great Again."

To make America great again means returning our nation to the point of greatness at which our country shone brighter than ever before. We can then build a new and more stable foundation to move America forward to an even greater place.

Unfortunately, millions of brainwashed Americans are lost and confused by the steady diet of fear porn and Anti-American propaganda delivered daily by the corporate fake news media. They couldn't even give you an answer as to when the last time America was truly great.

I believe that America was at the peak of its power, economically, culturally, and in the sheer level of national pride as one unified nation, at one specific point in modern history. Ironically, for today's Democrats and even some Republicans, that point of greatness was an era they once hailed as "A Time For Greatness" when the youngest and most vigorous presidential candidate since Teddy Roosevelt rose to the office of the presidency in 1960.

CHAPTER 4

The Last Time America was Great

"I GET A WARM FEELING WHEN I RE-MEMBER THE IDEALISM OF THE KENNEDYS. I'D LIKE TO SEE THAT SPIRIT REKINDLED IN WASHINGTON."

- DONALD TRUMP (2000)

Admittedly, Millennials and Zoomers were born a few decades too late and thus did not personally witness the magical times often referred to as "Camelot." However, they were not born yesterday, either. History has made evident that the last period in which our country was truly exceptional in every sense of the word was those thousand bright and sunny days when President John Fitzgerald Kennedy was in the Oval Office.

Kennedy ran for the presidency as the youngest presidential candidate in history. His slogan was "A Time For Greatness," to get the country moving forward again. He ran because he believed in the unlimited potential to which our innate freedom offered the United States, and her people the fuel to propel us forward. As with Lincoln, JFK fully understood our responsibility to our sacred American heritage as heirs of that first revolution. Therefore, he articulated the infinite potential of freedom with brilliance and tremendous energy.

Instead of making empty promises that he alone would never be able to deliver, Kennedy challenged the American people "to ask not what their country could do for them but what they could do for their country".

His call was to the young at heart, regardless of age, and to the spirit of America, regardless of one's partisan affiliation. The goal was lasting and consistent progress and forward movement, as pioneers and explorers, to seize and ultimately conquer the new frontiers of the 60s.

Upon his victory over Vice President Richard Nixon, the country he inherited from President Dwight D. Eisenhower was exceptional in every sense. Despite having faced recessions in the previous decade, this was a country at the absolute peak of her power, culturally, militarily, and economically. Most importantly, it was a time when the American Dream was still very much alive and well, and with it that timeless revolutionary and innately American spirit that birthed this nation.

As president, JFK was focused on solving the most significant problems, and surmounting the roadblocks hindering the United States from achieving its full potential. The elimination of poverty was high on that list. Thus, Kennedy sought to get the economy moving forward again by cutting burdensome and growth stifling taxes.

JFK understood that, "A rising tide lifts all boats." Therefore, he knew putting more money back into the pockets of the American people was the only way to expand the middle class and grow the American economy. Like every one of our most celebrated presidents, he was undoubtedly an example of what many today would consider America First. He once said, "Not first if, but, or when, but first."

As a staunch anti-communist, JFK desperately wanted to prove to the world that the United States, firing on all cylinders as a genuinely free market economy and society, was vastly superior in every way to communism and the oppressive Soviet Union.

In terms of foreign policy, JFK, as leader of the free world, took his role just as seriously as the role he took in the armed forces, among his fellow members of America's greatest generation. Therefore, building our military to full capacity to defend our national interests and keep America safe was both unavoidable and his highest priority as commander in chief.

Unlike many others, of his time and after him, JFK viewed other free nations of the world not as adversaries to conquer and exploit but as partners for progress. Thus, he brilliantly used the United States' position in the world to do humanity's heavy lifting, by advocating vigorously for all nations to put aside their disputes and pursue peace to avoid nuclear annihilation.

For example, take the Cuban Missile Crisis, when Kennedy famously prevented the imminent threat of a devastating nuclear exchange with the Soviets. Some see this move as appeasement; however, they must understand how close our nation was to nuclear war with the Soviet Union. They must also recognize that Kennedy was a man who endured the horrors of war himself, as it tragically claimed his own brother's life. Therefore, the last thing President Kennedy wanted was for the United States to risk destruction when his sole focus was advancing our country here at home.

Instead, he believed that constant competition among sovereign nations would provide the US and humanity with far more substantial and lasting benefits. JFK was not just your run of the mill placeholder president; his courage, vigor, and vision were larger than life. So too was his understanding of history.

To Kennedy, history would only remember leaders who dared to step outside of the status quo because they know in their hearts that it is the only way to move forward. His focus was on building for the future, not looking back to the past. Like all the greats before him, he knew that was the only means to lead, and the only way to move forward to something better.

Kennedy's brand of leadership was in a select category from the beginning of his political career. It was not in his nature to get stuck in petty partisan arguments intended to divide us or close himself off to new ideas. A voracious reader and constant spectator of history, JFK was fully knowledgeable of America's innate identity, purpose, responsibility in the world, and his fellow citizens.

John Kennedy believed that one's citizenship to our country meant more than just celebrating national holidays. To him, our citizenship was a sacred duty to contribute to society's betterment by simply doing one's best every day as American citizens. No matter who you are, what you look like, and what you do for a living, we have the God-given freedoms to make our lives anything we so choose. Therefore, no matter what path our citizens decided to take, giving maximum effort in our daily lives made the country better.

I am sure you will notice that Americans of all ages, colors, creeds, and political affiliates love JFK to this very day. Like President Lincoln, we all know that JFK was one of the very best presidents for his good and noble intentions.

He challenged all Americans to look within themselves and find the strength to be the best version of themselves, to look forward instead of looking behind, and demonstrate both courage and calm in the face of newness, instead of giving in to the fear of the unknown and thus choosing comfortable inaction.

Unfortunately, due to the ill will, greed, and shortsighted nature of self-interested people, the flame he lit was extinguished prematurely. That lively, vigorous, and noble leader left this earth with a mission unfulfilled. Still, he was successful in formulating the template for that sound and particularly modern brand of leadership. Many years after his death, the means of lifting that proverbial "sword in the stone" is still there for those who look close enough to find it, and liftable for the one mentally strong, and driven by a purpose great enough to bear the burdens of pulling it.

More than any other time, aside from the current season of history in which we live, JFK's America was capable of anything, even moving forward, beyond peace and war, beyond rich and poor, beyond left vs. right, and on to something better.

All those things Kennedy gave his life for, the quest of guiding our American experience forward, for he knew that the potential was there, and the timing was right. He understood the big picture and felt it his duty as president to articulate it to the American people.

Perhaps our nation would be in a far different place today had he not lost his life. However, I believe with all my heart that today John F. Kennedy would be a Republican and a supporter of Donald J. Trump. Let us remember that it was

Kennedy himself who said to the American people, "Let us not seek the Democrat answer or the Republican answer, but the right answer."

JFK's vigorous idealism is something Democrats, Republicans, and all Americans have longed for since his tragic death. Trump has undoubtedly utilized JFK's style as a template for his innate brand of leadership. That majestic time represented the kind of America we are striving to achieve again, thanks to Donald J. Trump. Only a great America is one that a new generation can move us forward, to that which Kennedy envisioned.

However, before we can move forward, we must examine another critical time when our nation was nearly back to greatness. Only when both of these eras are understood, will we fully comprehend how Donald J. Trump was able to bring America full circle.

CHAPTER 5

The Reagan Revolution

"REAGAN HAD CONFIDENCE, AND THE WORLD RESPECTED HIM FOR IT. THEY KNEW HE MEANT BUSINESS. TODAY, IT SEEMS WE DO EVERYTHING HALF-HEARTEDLY, UNSURE OF OURSELVES."

- DONALD TRUMP (2000)

Like President Kennedy, America's 40th President, Ronald Reagan, was a proud patriot, whose unshakable confidence and innate awareness of America's timeless revolutionary spirit and principles combined with his inherent gift of flawless communication, made him into a figure larger than life. Therefore, he too was proficient in cutting through party lines by speaking directly to the heart and soul of America and her people.

Unlike the privileged and well to do Kennedy, Reagan came from very humble beginnings, from serving our country in the military, to working in a sporting goods store, to sportscasting, followed by building a life as a successful and well known Hollywood actor.

Thus, even before entering the political arena, Ronald Reagan was already living breathing proof of the American Dream. Moreover, he knew full well that all American citizens had the potential to rise to any height they wished through hard work and perseverance. To him, this ability was innately American, and a gift from God himself and therefore believed our leaders and citizens had the sacred responsibility to protect and guard it with their lives.

From his earliest days in politics, he was fully aware that the deep underlying issues in our country stemmed from our government becoming too big, bloated, and inept.

He believed our founder's sacrifices gave every American citizen the ability to achieve success, as long as our nation's timeless principles continued to survive. Reagan knew freedom was the key and defined the infinite potential for America and her citizens to achieve the greatness for which we are all destined.

Therefore, he perhaps unknowingly expanded upon Kennedy's heroic call to seek the right answer and accept the responsibility for the future, in a speech that defined his political career in 1964, while presenting then presidential candidate Barry Goldwater to the Republican National Convention.

We now refer to that speech as "A Time for Choosing" when Reagan inferred that; "You and I are told increasingly we have to choose between left or right. Well, I'd like to suggest there is no such thing as a left or a right. There's only an up or down, [up] man's old-aged dream, the ultimate in individual freedom consistent with law and order, or down to the ant heap of totalitarianism."

Up and down. Forward and Backward. Like President Kennedy, Ronald Reagan knew that the road to progress was choosing to do what was right and move the country forward. To him, it was evident that choosing between a left and a right was not the same as choosing between an up and a down. Like JFK, he understood this.

As a profoundly proud American citizen, who lived the American Dream firsthand, he recognized that our nation's founders and greatest leaders championed freedom, liberty, personal responsibility because they enabled forward movement. Reagan believed wholeheartedly in the infinite potential of America's spirit and articulated it masterfully in his brand of leadership.

Thus, when campaigning for the presidency, he ran on the slogan to "Make America Great Again". What propelled him to victory over the weak incumbent Democrat President Jimmy Carter in the 1980 election, was his innate understanding of America's potential and the state of our nation at that time.

He coupled this with his ability to articulate the timeless principles that made America great in the first place. He knew full well that America had fallen from the greatness that we not only once enjoyed, but he also recognized that our federal government had become too big, bloated, corrupt and inept, and thus unable to meet the needs of the American people.

Therefore, as president, he championed the same hardline approach to communism as JFK, rigorously pushed to rebuild our military and kept the peace through superior military strength. He also used the same proven to work economic method of cutting taxes and deregulating American businesses, to put more money back into the pockets of the American people and grow the economy.

Ultimately, the results rebuilt America back to the peak of military power, a booming economy second to none anywhere in the world, and a country with citizens having more opportunities than ever before, now believing in the infinite potential of freedom and themselves once again.

Ronald Reagan once said, "America is too great to dream small dreams." Throughout his incredible life, the "Gipper" never did. Unfortunately, the years that were to follow his bright and sunny tenure in the Oval Office became dark and grim for America and her people.

In the last days of his life, Reagan saw that innately American ability to dream big dreams start to chip and fall away as a result of narrow-mindedness, self-interest, and importance, as well as greed and short-sightedness.

After Reagan departed the oval office, the tremendous progress to which his administration had made for America and her citizens began to evaporate quickly, while the norm and the mood had changed for the following presidents; leadership itself became a charade, and leaders became pretenders.

These were trends that trickled down into all corners of government in all 50 states. America had professional politicians running and winning elected office, but very few genuine leaders with the courage to chase and continue the crusade which JFK and Reagan dedicated their lives to achieve.

Instead of all-American leaders like John F. Kennedy and Ronald Reagan, America received more and more pretenders with a severe lack of understanding and failure to grasp the ever-elusive big picture with which only America's most immeasurable observed so clearly.

It became virtually taboo in American politics to lead for the big picture sense and put this country, and all of her people's future, first and foremost above anything. For leading that way, the right way, is undoubtedly not the easy way. Like Lincoln and Kennedy, Ronald Reagan too, was shown that with a bullet.

Indeed, playing the long game by choosing to do what is right, and ultimately to set the American people up for a better future, takes patience and the willingness to sacrifice political expedience. Only America's most significant leaders have the mental toughness to lead in such a way, even when no one is watching, aside from history and God himself.

Real leaders like Reagan and JFK do not care who gets the credit, as long as the work gets done and America is made all the better. They were big picture thinkers like our founders and thus played the long game because they knew that America would be better for it in the grand scheme of things.

These leaders are rare, and unfortunately, do not come around often, but we all know it when they do. That explains why America has been waiting for the next JFK since 1963, and the next Reagan since 1988, both of whom often quoted the infinite wisdom of Thomas Jefferson and Abraham Lincoln in their speeches.

Why did they do that?

Not because of his political party, but because it was Lincoln himself who was inspired by the commonsensical pragmatism and revolutionary principles of Jefferson. This pragmatic approach and these guiding principles are what Jefferson used to guide his fellow citizens forward, on freedoms road to progress. The truth is, our country's forward motion has occurred because of people, principles, and ideas, not platforms, and not the parties themselves.

Reagan was a Democrat early on in his lifetime because he inherently believed in the principles laid out by Thomas Jefferson.

One factor that ties Reagan and Lincoln together, aside from their membership to the Republican Party, was their mutual respect and admiration of Thomas Jefferson, one of the most significant pillars and stewards of America's sacred founding principles.

Reagan saw the truth that the parties themselves were just vehicles for great men and women to champion our nation's most sacred principles, as those principles were the recipe for prosperity and greatness.

All of our history's most treasured leaders stand out from the pack, like our courageous founders, unlike those who stand in its shadow. That is the reason why Honest Abe, JFK, and the Gipper, serve as shining stars, who not only define the parties, but guide the people themselves.

They do so because they transcend politics and make a lasting difference, which is far more significant than those who merely tow the party line. They are bigger than the parties themselves.

Simply put, they are AMERICAN presidents. That is why AMERICANS in both parties, and even lifelong independents, look to their timeless leadership and inspiring words for guidance to this very day.

Like Reagan, our 45th president is no different, as we will discuss in great detail in the next section.

CHAPTER 6

The Very Stable Genius

"HERE'S THE BOTTOM LINE: ANY POLIT-ICAL LEADER WHO WON'T FACE THE FUTURE HEAD-ON IS PUTTING THE AMERICAN DREAM AT RISK"
- DONALD TRUMP (2000)

The American people have endured many decades of waiting, hoping, and praying for an all-American leader in the mold of a John Kennedy or Ronald Reagan. Unfortunately, for all those hard-working and God-fearing Americans like my grandparents, electing such a leader was inconceivable, because our government had become so broken and its leaders so self-serving and corrupt.

As my beloved grandfather told me many times growing up, America needed an OUTSIDER who was self-made and understood not only how the system worked from the outside, but just how rotten to the core it was on the inside. A DISRUPTER, who would tell the brutally honest to God's truth, no matter how uncomfortable, and work tirelessly to set things right again. Our country did not need another partisan puppet, but an inherently AMERICAN president.

What exactly does that mean?

According to JFK, "The American by his nature, is optimistic, he is an inventor, and a builder, who builds best when called upon to build greatly."

In a nutshell, that is Donald J. Trump, who, unlike Kennedy, nor any president before him, was the ultimate political outsider. He did not make his way in the cesspool that is the Washington DC swamp, but rather by building incredible architecture and making "Yuge" deals in the business world.

The experience Trump procured in the world of business allowed him to observe and understand how the DC swamp operated. Therefore, he knew what to do by the time he took it upon himself to leave his life of luxury behind and yield his talents and innate expertise to his country and his fellow citizens. Trump didn't have to do this. He could have easily chosen to continue running his business while enjoying his beautiful family and fortune. But his love for his country and sincere concern for its future ultimately propelled him to begin the historic effort to "Drain the Swamp" and replace its slimy creatures with freedom-loving American patriots.

All Americans must realize that President Trump is just what the doctor ordered to fix our broken country. Simply put, he was tailor-made for this specific window of our nation's history, much like Honest Abe. The latter disrupted his day's broken political system and brought America full circle by combining the best traits among the greatest of his predecessors with his own, thus re-setting the table of America and its politics for years to come.

Our very own "Honest" Don has utilized that method, by combining the idealism of Kennedy, the strong and principled leadership of Reagan, with precisely the straight talk Lincoln used so many years ago to be the transformative leader America both needs and deserves.

For these reasons, I have been a Trump supporter since he rode down those escalators in 2015 with his beautiful wife. Throughout the 2016 presidential primary debates, I knew he was the only one who could defeat Hillary.

President Donald J. Trump said on February 5, 2019, when giving his second State of the Union in front of Congress and the American people, "We meet tonight, at a moment of unlimited potential." Due to the tremendous progress Donald J. Trump has made for America during just his first term in office, yes, indeed, we were and are today, living and meeting at a time of unlimited potential.

Do you know how?

By seeking the right answers instead of merely the partisan stamped Republican or Democrat answers, as JFK suggested to the American people in the 60s. By making decisions and formulating solutions based upon an up-down axis, rather than a left and a right, as Ronald Reagan first spoke of in his unforgettable 1964 speech, "A Time For Choosing." And yes, by not carrying out a Republican Agenda or a Democrat agenda that only benefits career politicians, but an "American agenda" that benefits the United States of America and its citizens.

Many said this particular State of the Union was by far the best speech president Trump had made up to that point while in office. Even the heavily biased mainstream media pundits loved it. Therefore, I would also assert that it will be one of the most defining of his presidency when all is said and done because he legitimately showed his cards, his genuine chosen brand of leadership. It is the same gold standard our founders intended for America's leaders to execute. It is rare, timeless, powerful, and its potential to deliver results is unlimited for those with the guts to adhere to the scrutiny that comes with it.

Like John F. Kennedy and Ronald Reagan, Trump's brand is one that knows no partisan boundaries, as it transcends politics, broken promises, and excuses. Trump knows, as JFK and

Reagan did, the "right answer" was "up or down," not Democrat and Republican, and neither left nor right. The direction that our founders intended for WE the American people, the heirs of that first revolution, was to move forward, not sideways nor backwards like the career politicians want us to believe.

The angry Democrats in America today, hate that he frequently mentions all of the promises he has kept as president. They are promises Democrats and RINO Republicans alike, had campaigned on for years on end. However, the difference is that Trump, and the Republicans in Congress who have bought into the America First Agenda, have delivered on them.

Our best leaders through history are the few who have led for all of the American people as a whole, as opposed to the many who chose to single us out by dividing us with identity politics and false labels.

In the modern era, our two most significant leaders of the past sixty years, presidents Kennedy and Reagan, not only empowered and united the American people but proposed solutions for all Americans alike, and ultimately delivered results. Unfortunately, nearly every elected leader who despises Trump, is often one who promised everything, but never delivered.

Their only concern seems to be serving themselves instead of the American people. They have failed for not chasing solutions to make right on their broken promises, and instead only chasing the guarantee of perpetual re-election.

They seem to be envious of this man, because he had never run for office in his life, became president, and has delivered "big league" on the promises they have spent their whole careers making and breaking.

Everything comes in threes, whether it is a great book series, films, and even eras of history. Trump has solidified his place in history with JFK and "The Gipper" during just his first term as president and has proven he was not the demagogue to which the Democrats and Never-Trumpers have labeled him. Like Lincoln before him, Trump has forever changed American politics by bringing our nation full circle. America finally has a president bringing ideas and themes of both parties together, a new gold standard of American leadership dedicated to transparency, authenticity, and above all else, results. We cannot accept anything less. Trump has set the bar high, and a new generation of Americans must hold every elected official to this new standard in this new decade, and all those to come.

CHAPTER 7

Behold a New Golden Standard

*"A GENUINE LEADER IS NOT A
SEARCHER FOR CONSENSUS, BUT A
MOLDER OF CONSENSUS."*

- DR. MARTIN LUTHER KING, JR.

All Americans, especially young Americans, must see the writing on the wall and start thinking in the big picture sense. We cannot accept anything less than we deserve in this critical decade of the 20s.

Now the American people have the much needed third piece to the puzzle, in Donald Trump, and thus have a new standard by which to hold our leaders. From now on, we can only accept those worthy of our time and tax dollars.

To recap: John F. Kennedy told us that, "We must not seek the Republican answer or the Democratic answer, but the right answer." Similarly, Ronald Reagan said that there was no left and right, only an up or a down. Now, Donald J. Trump told us all these years later that there was no Republican agenda or Democrat agenda, only the American peoples' agenda. Victory was not winning for one's party but for one's country.

All Americans must know that these are timeless and universal concepts and serve a historical purpose. Our country deserves this standard of leadership, and moving forward, we deserve all of our leaders to say these things and genuinely adhere to them and believe them, not just sometimes but all the time.

The success of our future hinges on us choosing leaders who lead for all of our people, who understand the big picture as our founders did, as did Lincoln and these three great men.

Those of us who already see the big picture know there is not and has never been a Democrat or Republican answer. We also know there is no "right or "left" through which our solutions must come.

We need leaders who KNOW and RESPECT that there is ONLY a right and wrong way of doing anything. Choosing what is morally right moves you and everyone forward while succumbing to selfishness, fear, or envy, and choosing the wrong thing will keep you stagnant or worse.

Having elected officials making poor decisions instead of doing the right thing as we expect them to do when we vote for them is how our country became so inherently broken in the first place. Now, Americans must demand only leaders for whom we can be sure will genuinely represent the interests of all the people they are elected to serve at every level of government.

The days of settling for pretenders who only wish to accumulate power, prestige, and wealth must end. We need leaders who will say no to fat-cat lobbyists and shady backroom donors because their sweetheart deals do nothing to advance the interests of our country and citizens.

America needs leaders who give the authority they receive upon attaining office right back to the people who elect them, by including them in the process of governing, and listening to their ideas and employing them.

The mentality of those who get elected to public office must change, as public servants are never above or superior to the people who put them there. The truth is that no one person can lead on their own; it takes a collective effort to make a real difference anywhere in this country and the world. At the end of the day, we are all the same.

For example, in every puzzle, no matter the size and scope of the picture, each piece comes together to complete the whole.

Among the individual parts, you will notice that some look similar, sure, but no one ever looks the same, as each one of them possesses a different function. What makes them all inherently the same is that each has a specific purpose and is vital to the ultimate goal, its completion.

The United States and the American people are no different.

This country itself is nothing more than an enormous and complex puzzle consisting of millions of pieces. Each piece (American citizen) represents an indispensable part with inherent talents, skills, ideas, and purposes, all of which perfectly fit into our collective citizenry, and are needed to complete the puzzle. As Americans, we don't look the same from one person to the next, but then again, neither do puzzle pieces. More importantly, our collective and shared citizenship as Americans and our membership to the human race is what connects us all equally.

Moving forward, we need leaders who can make the American people understand that we all have the same common goals as collective pieces of the American puzzle. That must be reinforced daily for those who do not see it. Even considering our differences, the goal of us all, and our country is greatness. We can no longer waste any more energy being petty; it is time we move forward, not look behind, and we must do so together.

The path forward is paved through a superior understanding of our nation's history, and now with the truth that is America's Perigon in our peripherals, we must analyze the current political climate and state of American politics going into the 2020 election.

In the old political climate, I would tell you it did not matter, as both parties were the same two sides of the same dirty coin, and before Trump, that was true.

Now, the picture is more apparent than ever before, and the Democrat Party has not only lost itself entirely, but they have become a significant threat to our nation's very survival.

CHAPTER 8

Today's Democrats

*"I THINK DEMOCRATS MADE A MIS-
TAKE RUNNING AWAY FROM LIBERAL-
ISM. LIBERALISM, UH, FRANKLIN
ROOSEVELT, HARRY TRUMAN, JOHN
AND ROBERT KENNEDY – THAT'S
WHAT THE DEMOCRATIC PARTY
OUGHT TO REACH FOR."*

- THEODORE C. SORENSON

Presidents Jefferson, Jackson, Wilson, Truman, Roosevelt,

and Kennedy, would be appalled to see what has become of what Ronald Reagan once referred to as "that once-great and honorable party." Today, it is even far worse than merely being a shadow of its former self; now, it is something else entirely.

The Democrat Party has moved rapidly and radically far beyond the furthermost reaches of the "left" wing to the edge of literal insanity. At this point, they have morphed into a violent anti-American hate group. Unfortunately, the party of Jefferson is lost forever, and he and his fellow founding fathers are very likely turning in their graves.

Thanks to the Clinton/Obama axis of evil, it has transformed into a party to which Vladimir Lenin, Joseph Stalin and Karl Marx would collectively flock to in droves. Whether one wants to define its current radical platform as Leninism, Communism, Marxism, or even place the term Democratic in front of Socialism, it is irrelevant. It all means the same thing, TYRANNY.

Today's Democrat Party is pushing hard to remake America into a dystopian society where the promise of opportunity and prosperity is nothing other than an afterthought. They want a society in chaos and ruin, where nothing is achievable for anyone who does not adhere to their false reality of lies. Even those who drink from the proverbial punch bowl will not know prosperity, because if the Democrats have their way, this country will be devoid of freedom, liberty, and order. As they demonstrated in their respective era of history, our founders would never have accepted any of this. That is preciously the reason they saw it imperative to break away from tyranny and oppression almost two and a half centuries ago. They chose to conduct an epic experiment to build a society upon the pillars of freedom, individual liberty, and justice under the law. Many generations of American's after them were thus free to pursue a life of meaning while chasing their innate version of the American dream. Now, the Democrat party is using every possible tool in their toolbox to trick young Americans into outright giving up their birthright.

Therefore, it is high time this generation, and all young Americans begin to recognize that freedom is not something we can barter with, nor ever take for granted.

In the words of Ronald Reagan: "Freedom is a fragile thing and is never more than one generation away from extinction. It is not ours by inheritance; it must be fought for and constantly defended by each generation, for it comes only once to a people."

For those among us who know this, we bear the responsibility of alerting those who do not.

The 2020 Democrat Party aims to brainwash Americans of every generation into not only resenting the gifts our founders made our birthright, but giving them up forever.

What will we receive in return?

A society held captive by the same type of tyranny our founders ran from in the first place.

These "Democratic" socialists call themselves progressives, but that is only to make their trap of tyranny look appealing to us. Glamorizing socialism in the name of "progress" and pushing a platform tailor-made for the destruction of our constitutional rights, civil liberties, and free-market capitalism is, in fact, the exact opposite of progress.

Therefore, the Democrat party is not the party of progress. Their actions have indicated they have no awareness whatsoever of what the term "progress" even means.

In all honesty, the Democrat Party's platform has not delivered anything resembling forward progress for America since Jack Kennedy was at the head of that party. Sadly, so many Americans cling to the false reality that this party is the same as it once was in the days of John and Robert F. Kennedy. The platform they championed highlighted the importance of hard work, earning a living, standing up for the American worker, and adhering to and protecting our constitutional rights and American values.

However, those who believe the modern Democrat Party embodies those concepts are living in a fantasy world. The contemporary iteration of the Democrat party and its leaders have bartered and wasted those principles just as they have their voters hopes, dreams, and tax dollars.

The fact is, after Kennedy's tragic murder, their platform was deeply corrupted and went to hell in a handbasket the moment Lyndon Baines Johnson took over as president in 1964. Every single new frontier program to which JFK worked so vigorously to get through Congress got hijacked, perverted, and ultimately rebranded into Johnsons Great Society.

Remember, this was the party in favor of slavery during the Civil War. This party supported Jim Crow, and it was the party of the Klu Klux Klan. Johnson did not care about Kennedy's historic Civil Rights Bill whatsoever. He only ensured it was passed through the Congress to gain the African American voting bloc for years to come. For so many years, Americans accepted the lie that the Democrat Party was the party of progress. Admittedly, it was in the days of the Kennedy's, but that was a short window of time.

For the past sixty years, the Democrat Party has been using every trick in the book to divide the American people and indoctrinate us with their fake humanitarian rhetoric, all of which is to win votes and win elections. They will do and say anything to blind us of the common citizenship to which all Americans share equally.

Because for them, Americans are nothing but voting blocs to exploit, and they will use anything from race, skin pigmentation, religion, socioeconomic status, or sexual orientation to blind us of the common citizenship to which we all share.

They continue promoting the myth that they are the party of progress. However, the reality is that they have not been for decades. On the other hand, the party of Honest Abe has come full circle due to America's Perigon. Thanks to Donald J. Trump, it again stands for the same principles he and our founders intended for the American people.

Therefore, it is again the party of progress and vehicle to greater prosperity. Before the rise of Trump, however, the party of Lincoln was in grave danger of suffering the same fate as the Whig Party, and America itself was facing destruction.

CHAPTER 9

Party of Progress

"I AM A REPUBLICAN, A BLACK, DYED IN THE WOOL REPUBLICAN, AND I NEVER INTEND TO BELONG TO ANY OTHER PARTY THAN THE PARTY OF FREEDOM AND PROGRESS"

\- FREDRICK DOUGLASS

The political climate of America in 2015 was eerily similar to the period just before our American Civil War. Two sets of parties that had become a shell of their former selves, with one leading the charge to shatter the American economy, divide our people, and ultimately destroy our nation. Thus, America required a unique kind of leader. One who could bring our country full circle and clear the table for a brand-new era in American politics just as we did all those years ago.

Abraham Lincoln rose to the occasion when he witnessed this same scenario with the Whig Party, and thus fashioned a brand new one that not only equaled the times but personified the same founding principles that forged our nation. The ending result was a new party founded on the concept of defending our birthright as American citizens and a vehicle to propel us forward.

In his wisdom, Lincoln knew that for America to accomplish this, the American people would need every one of those innate and sacred freedoms and timeless principles. Therefore, he set a brand-new standard for one hundred years of American politics.

It was a standard which legendary Republican leaders like Teddy Roosevelt, Dwight D. Eisenhower, and Ronald Reagan not only adhered to but combined with new innovative solutions to move America further toward greatness and lasting prosperity. Like Lincoln before them, they stayed true to that timeless and innately American spirit and the principles which founded this nation. Most of all, they put our nation's interests and those of our people FIRST above all else.

After President Ronald Reagan left office, however, the Washington swamp and the GOP became overly contaminated with greedy, self-serving career politicians. For nearly thirty years, their broken promises and failed solutions coupled with the willingness to sacrifice our freedoms and individual liberties made them indistinguishable from the Democrats.

A century after our American Civil War and that same Grand Old Party to which Lincoln established had found itself in the same place as the Whig Party before it. Therefore, another transformative leader was needed to bring about the same result as Lincoln did all those years ago. By the grace of God almighty, we got one in President Donald J. Trump, the catalyst for America's Perigon, who brought our country, her politics, our timeless revolutionary spirit, and the Republican Party full circle.

Once again, the party of "Honest" Abraham Lincoln is the party of freedom, the constitution, and the American worker, of unlimited opportunities, social justice, and mutual tolerance. In short, it is the party to which our courageous founders would approve, the party of progress, principle, and the vehicle to forward movement.

Thanks to President Trump, the GOP has come back to being AMERICA FIRST. Once again, the platform adheres to our most timeless and sacred principles, while also vigorously defending our Constitutional Rights.

President Trump has stayed true and kept more promises than any politician in American political history and is not only draining the wildly corrupt Washington swamp but also championing a new standard of excellence, transparency, and results.

Speaking of results, under his watch, America has accomplished more than ever before.

Under the leadership of President Trump, we have taken an outdated and depleted military and transformed it into the most robust, modern, and technologically advanced iteration in our country's history. Thus, our country was able to obliterate ISIS and put radical Islamic terror on the run.

President Trump brought a broken American economy back from the brink of destruction by utilizing the same proven economic method as presidents John F. Kennedy and Ronald Reagan. He passed the most significant tax cuts in the history of our nation and had the sense to make right on his promises to remove the United States out of the job-killing "Free trade" agreements like NAFTA and TPP. Like no president before him, Trump dared to demand fair trade deals with the rest of the world, stood up to China by forcing strategic tariffs to balance our trade deficit, and made the United States not only independent in terms of energy but the most abundant exporter in the world once again.

The results were record-breaking stock market highs, the lowest unemployment rates ever recorded for all Americans, including minorities, and ultimately the most robust and booming economy in our nation's history.

Aside from the surging economy, he passed legislation to reform our outdated and highly corrupt justice system. He fought to secure our borders against gangs and human trafficking, stood up for veterans, law enforcement professionals, and our people of faith. Trump also got behind our most treasured allies around the world whose values we share, which he demonstrated by moving the Jewish embassy to Jerusalem. The list goes on and on.

Today, Honest Abe would be mighty proud that his "Grand Old Party" has finally come full circle and pleased with the leader at the helm. Donald Trump has delivered more results for the American people than any other president, especially for minorities, and in just one term in office, perhaps even more than Lincoln himself. Simply put, the high level at which Trump has delivered for the American people has set a brand-new standard that has challenged his fellow Republican leaders to do the same. It has also inspired millions of young Americans to want to join the fight to make a difference themselves.

Trump's many successes and delivered promises are the standards to which we must hold all of our leaders. They are the starting point upon which a new generation may use as a model to continue the fight to drain the swamp, as the fight is far from over.

Only when we observe a government completely drained of career politicians, lies, and broken promises can we then replace it with a new foundation of leadership. One built on integrity, transparency, and commitment to delivering results above all else. We the people deserve these traits in all of our elected officials, and the days of Americans having to question if they are present or not, must end for good.

Being committed to our nation's most timeless principles, such as faith, freedom, individual liberty, and free thinking is not in any way detrimental to forward movement. Nor does it mean we cannot formulate new solutions and undergo bold and daring projects. On the contrary, those things only serve as the safeguards for us to push our ideas and American innovations in technology, art, culture, and everything under the sun to their absolute limit. They are also the tools by which we will then break those limits and push them even further.

Every American citizen should be proud of their heritage and want our nation to be first. We can only vote for and elect leaders who put AMERICA FIRST, and I mean ALL the American people, not just some of them.

Thankfully, the next generation of Americans can sleep well at night, knowing we have dynamic leaders like Congressman Matt Gaetz of Florida, who has been fighting side-by-side with our great president on the front lines of freedom to bring our country back to greatness and secure our future.

From the very beginning, he and his colleagues in the House Freedom Caucus have demonstrated the courage to have our president's back and defend our nation's most timeless principles. Despite how much these patriots have accomplished for the American people, still, Gaetz, and his freedom caucus need more help in this eternal struggle to preserve America and our future.

That is why we must choose vigorous America First candidates running for office all over this nation, who demonstrate the tenacity and enthusiasm to not only support our president, but also make a real difference, and ensure this party continues to be a force for lasting prosperity throughout this new decade.

Together, we can achieve anything and build a future worthy of America's infinite potential. But we must understand that the success or failure of that future hinges on us, and how we choose to approach this critical election, as the choices we make now will determine the road our country ultimately takes as we settle into this new decade of the 20s.

The Republican Party under Donald J. Trump is the best chance to defend freedom, and in the words of John F. Kennedy, "The road to progress is freedoms road"; therefore, it should not be a difficult one for any American to make.

Unfortunately, his Democrat party gave up on both a long time ago. Now, they are working every day to shatter nearly 250 years of societal progress and destroy the most productive economic system this world has ever known.

More than ever, our freedom, liberty, and future are at higher risk today than at any other time in history. Suppose the Democrats succeed in carrying out their ultimate goals. In that case, they will fundamentally destroy this generation's ability to build and achieve the future we all desire and rightfully deserve.

WE THE PEOPLE cannot allow this to happen, not if you and I have anything to say about it, anyway.

In this next chapter, we will break through their fog of lies with facts and straight talk. The same recipe Donald J. Trump successfully utilized to win the hearts and minds of the American people and put us back on the fast track to greatness.

However, for us to fully get back there, young Americans must free themselves from the mental prison where the left has entrapped them.

CHAPTER 10

The Party of Tyranny

"THE HISTORY OF THE DEMOCRAT
PARTY IS ONE OF SLAVERY, SECESSION,
SEGREGATION, AND NOW SOCIALISM."
- ALLEN WEST

Today's Democrats are laser-focused on three things, destroying our American economy, getting re-elected endlessly, and of course, defeating and humiliating our president. To accomplish these goals, they will do and say anything. From brainwashing the American people to resent their innately American freedoms, inciting violence, hostility, and division amongst our citizens with identity politics and yes, even canceling and re-writing our American history, indeed, everything is fair game.

They stick to their "Big lie" technique, which entails telling the same falsehoods repeatedly, so in time, people believe them as fact. Ironically, this was the same tactic Hitler used to deceive the German people during World War II.

Like him, the Democrats talk out of all sides of their mouths, day in and day out, preaching that THEY are the party that champions equality, tolerance, fairness, social justice, and humanitarianism. Yet, the exact OPPOSITE is true. In the real world, they don't care about any of these things whatsoever.

They utilize these concepts as masks to hide behind, and tools through which to dupe and pigeonhole the American people into categories based on appearance, sexual orientation, religious beliefs, and socioeconomic status. Collectively, they use these cards to segregate our citizenry and thereby slice and dice us into small groups, instead of the united country we are supposed to be. But they don't want us united. To them, we are more valuable divided, broken, and ignorant of our shared citizenship and humanity.

They believe the American people can be narrowed down into single voting blocs to exploit for votes and campaign donations to achieve perpetual re-election and power. For example, take the 2020 Democrat presidential nominee, former Vice President, Joe Biden, a lifelong career politician who wants nothing more than to destroy our freedoms, liberty, and country.

Like many professional politicians in Washington, Biden sold his soul to communist China quite a long time ago, and now he wants to sell off his own country and finish what Hillary Clinton could not. He had a front-row seat while the Clinton-Obama crime syndicate and two party-duopoly were paving the way for America's demise and securing big fat payoffs and sweetheart deals for their elitist friends and political donors.

Sure, they can preach free trade all they want, but free trade was not fair trade, and they sacrificed the American Dream and our middle class to the globalist cabal. Their goal was to use Communist China as a model to mold their policies that weaken our freedoms, economy, and push our nation toward eventual collapse, only to have it reborn again as their ideal 1984 socialist utopia.

Today, those goals have not only remained unchanged, they have accelerated. Unfortunately, millions of Americans, many of them young, fall hook line and sinker for the divisive and ruthless tactics of these political hacks.

How do Democrats get young people to buy into their lies?

They peddle career politicians at the presidential level who adhere to the same old playbook; the one that promises the American people more security in exchange for bigger government, higher taxes, and the further erosion of our civil liberties. Meanwhile, they rely on radical extremists in the Congress, with energy, charisma, and the high capacity to speak the opposite of truth without remorse, to do their heavy lifting.

At the same time, they knowingly deceive them into believing that the best possible future they could ever possess is one of socialism, where everything is free, everything is lovely, and those who don't think so are racist.

In reality, the ideal future for the Democrats is one utterly devoid of freedom, liberty, opportunity, religion, and privacy. It is one where they are all re-elected continuously. They will do and say anything to make it sound like the opposite, whatever it takes to keep their power and do the bidding of their masters who ensure their re-election.

What are thy masters bidding?

All of them want full-on globalism, the destruction of our nation's sovereignty, and constitutional rights because then they will succeed in fulfilling their dream, to obliterate the infinite potential of the American people and America itself.

Why?

To accumulate as much money, power, and influence as possible. Despite how much these globalists already have, and how they got it, no amount is ever enough for these people. Therefore, they will use every tool available to destroy their political enemies (conservatives and people of faith) to ensure they get what they want.

Democrats and their globalist handlers desperately want mass censorship of our free speech on television, in our communities, and especially on social media, which they now have monopolized. In schools, they want to belittle young people in the exclusively left-leaning halls of academia where our timeless American principles, sacred values, and free thought are considered either hate crimes or racist.

Oh, but they want us to be equal, right?

Wrong.

They can preach equality until they are blue in the face, and they do.

But their version of equality is about as "equal" as the broken nations whose people suffered and perished like in the failed Soviet Union, Cuba, and Venezuela. These societies have only two classes, rich and poor, no in-between where the magic of the American Dream happens. Thus no opportunities for people to achieve their unlimited human potential as we have enjoyed here in the United States.

The Democrats version of living isn't truly living, but merely existing in misery under the thumb of an all-powerful central government with no way out of oppression nor a way to move up the ladder of society.

To them, it's more appealing to have an American working-class broken, desperate, and held firmly in place through excessive taxation that will make the legendary American middle-class nothing more than a relic of the past. They want freedom for the ultra-elite and socialism for the rest of "Deplorable" America.

Indeed, they want us to be equal, equally weak, worthless, and utterly miserable. Aside from a few exceptions, the Democrats have always been the party of tyranny. Their love of socialism, the modern form of slavery, is no exception. Accepting it would cancel everything our nation has achieved since the days of Lincoln, and fundamentally indicate a death sentence for the United States of America.

CHAPTER 11

Why Socialism is a Death Sentence for America

"SOCIALSIM IS A PHILOSOPHY OF FAIL-URE, THE CREED OF IGNORANCE, AND THE GOSPEL OF ENVY, IT'S INHERENT VIRTUE IS THE EQUAL SHARING OF MIS-ERY."

- WINSTON CHURCHILL

The ideology of socialism is unsustainable; it produces no

wealth for the average working-class American citizen because it leaves no room for advancement nor the hope of class mobility. Adopting socialism would be a death sentence for America and her citizens.

In a socialist society, there is no freedom, individual liberty, or the opportunity to advance yourself and others. No matter how trendy the Democrat Party has made socialism appear to young Americans, they don't understand that it would require trading in their American Dream for a horrific nightmare. Those who endured the brutal and oppressive Soviet Union lived that nightmare every day, as do those who live in Communist China.

The Chinese have done an excellent job buying off the Democrat Party and Silicon Valley and using pop culture to glamorize socialism to naive American consumers. However, the truth is that those Chinese citizens are not satisfied nor prospering, and very likely wish they were living in the United States.

The vast majority of them live in utter hell, working 18-hour days in factories that produce OUR American goods. These are human beings working themselves to death in these literal slave labor facilities, who are not living life to the fullest, but merely existing at the mercy of their government and ruling class. Sadly, the suicide rate continues to rise, while their bigwigs in government and government-controlled mega corporations get more affluent and want for very little.

Again, with socialism, there is NO class mobility. There are only two classes, one rich and the other poor.

The upper class includes a small group of wealthy elites who enjoy a never-ending life of luxury, as long as they agree to enrich and adhere to the all-powerful central government. Simultaneously, the people in the lower class spend their lives breaking their backs in service to them. Unlike free-market capitalism, there is no way up the ladder, because a socialist nation locks the door for its people to achieve a higher socioeconomic status and greater prosperity.

The end result of socialism in America would be to give up our middle class and inherently destroy the American Dream. Adopting such a model here in our country would be foolish and not conducive to advancing progress and greater prosperity for our society.

Every country is different, societally, culturally, and economically. However, history has demonstrated that the ideology and economic model of socialism will fail miserably, again and again, no matter the country that tries it.

Therefore, why would Americans be foolish enough to think it would produce a different result here in the United States, when we already have a society that has produced the most effective model to generate wealth and lasting prosperity for our country and its citizens?

In the words of Donald J. Trump, "America will never be a socialist country."

We need our leaders to make productive policies structured around the ultimate goal; to put America and her people first. The American people do not need leaders who champion policies that take away from them what they need to live their lives to the fullest every day and be productive citizens.

Implementing newer and more innovative solutions is critical to our nation and our people's upward movement toward infinite potential and greater prosperity. However, we cannot execute any of those new solutions, without considering those ideas and principles required to move forward in the first place. That is where today's Democrats have it all wrong.

Many self-described "Democratic" socialists in America today have no clue what the ideology of socialism even means nor what it entails for them and our country. Sadly, they believe what they believe because mainstream media, entertainment, music, and pop culture, have all glamorized socialism as this beautiful new and trendy idea, and that Republicans, conservatives, and people of faith are living in the past by clinging onto old ideas. In reality, the truth is the exact opposite.

Sure, the ideals to which we believe and hold dear are rather old, but then again, so is socialism. No matter how hard the Democrat Party tries to rebrand it as new, that fact will never change. Nor will they change the fact that it is a lousy "old" idea, and one this generation and all those after cannot afford. Socialism and its tyrannical faulty ideas and policies would mean the death of society and halt the potential for a prosperous journey through this new decade.

Instead, we need those old ideals that are TIMELESS, such as faith, freedom, individual liberty, and personal responsibility, as we move into the future. They are worth our effort to preserve, as they are the foundation on which innovation, forward progress, and greater prosperity are made possible. As we settle into this new decade, we must not be afraid to hold onto those timeless and priceless ideals. Socialism is certainly not one of them.

Unfortunately, the bigger picture is right there for today's Democrats to see, and they don't even know it.

CHAPTER 12

Don't be Afraid to Fight for the Old Ideals!

"YOU WILL NEVER KNOW HOW MUCH IT HAS COST MY GENERATION TO PRE-SERVE YOUR FREEDOM. I HOPE YOU WILL MAKE A GOOD USE OF IT."

— JOHN ADAMS

The bigger picture that eludes so many Americans, is that we already possess everything we need to be successful in our daily lives as citizens, thanks to the United States Constitution, and the foresight of our brilliant founders. Therefore, today, every generation of Americans must realize what they acquired upon birth.

That sacred gift is their citizenship to a society like no other in the history of the world. It is one founded on the pillars of freedom, liberty, and justice under the law. Such a culture is unique and stands apart from the long history of the world. Unlike many other advanced nations, America is a place where one is free to pursue the destiny of his or her choosing. On the journey toward one's purpose, our country provides its citizens with every tool to make their dreams a reality. Our founders wanted those tools so badly they fought a revolution to achieve them, and when they did, they knew protecting them would be a tall order.

Today, with all the critical issues our country faces, the most pressing and urgent among them is the one that has remained since the days of our founders. That is our perpetual struggle of ensuring freedoms survival.

Every day, our sacred constitutional rights, are under continuous assault by enemies both within and outside our borders. Our adversaries see their priceless worth and comprehend their ability to grant the American people full access to our reservoir of unlimited human potential. They know full well that without them, we cannot, and will not, achieve our destiny, nor go forward as a nation and a people.

That is why we must do what is required to retain them.

John F. Kennedy once said, "We, in this country, must be willing to do battle for old ideas that have proved their value with the same enthusiasm that people do for new ideas and creeds."

Undoubtedly, all these years later, Americans of all ages must wake up and see the big picture right in front of our faces. We must resume and fight every bit of that epic battle for the old ideals. Faith, freedom, liberty, and the pursuit of one's happiness and greater prosperity has allowed America to rise to heights no other nation or people have known.

Today, we desperately need those ideals, and we always will, because those old ideals, which are our sacred and timeless American values, are the very foundation and bedrock on which advancement and forward movement are even possible. We have to combine those old ideals with our passion and with fresh faces and loud voices to ensure they stand the test of time.

That is how we will articulate brand new solutions to solve our nation's biggest problems weighing on our country, preventing us from moving forward. We need new leaders who will not be beholden to the failures and broken promises of yesterday. Now more than ever, all Americans, especially those who are young and those forever young at heart, must WAKE UP and join the historic effort to move America forward.

In the coming months and years, we will need all Americans of every generation to muster the courage and be willing to battle for those old ideals and defend them. Because within those old ideals is the guarantee of our very survival and the fuel needed for us to rise and soar as high as America's infinite potential will allow.

Those ideals secure our birthright as American citizens to soar as high as we choose and achieve any and every dream no matter its size and scope. It is one that belongs to every American citizen equally, regardless of political affiliation, color, creed, or sexual orientation. We are all God's children and citizens of this Republic. Therefore, we all have the same infinite potential and American destiny.

But in this brand-new era where God and history have placed us, we must not stoop to those who seek to take our nation's most timeless principles and freedoms away from us. Yes, we must fight and push back against those who seek to destroy the American dream, but we cannot do so with violence and prejudice.

The only way our fellow Americans will stop undermining our collective American destiny is by bombarding them with facts through constructive and passionate discussion. Although we must be respectful and patient with them, we must persist in presenting them with the truth. That is the only way to attain the sort of future America is truly capable of, when firing on all cylinders.

All Americans must see and process what has indeed happened over the past four years, which has undoubtedly been the rebirth of America's spirit and infinite potential. Thanks to Donald J. Trump, the catalyst for America's Perigon, this is now our reality. Those who still don't get it, or see the big picture, must be educated by those who do know and do see it, as they deserve to know what is on the line and what we are working so tirelessly to achieve.

Ultimately, the goal is to transition our country back to genuine greatness successfully. But to do so, we need all Americans to recognize the priceless worth of those old ideals. Also, we will need every one of those old ideals to protect and propel us to the future we deserve.

There is a reason why America has to be great. Only a great America can provide its citizens with an equal opportunity to maximize the infinite potential at our fingertips, and to live our lives free and independently in our constant pursuit of personal happiness and fulfillment, and regardless of fashion or convention, achieve the life of our dreams. Ultimately, a great America will enable us to move forward to a place more excellent than anything we can imagine.

CHAPTER 13

Moving Forward Again

"IT'S NOT ABOUT WHAT IT IS, IT'S
ABOUT WHAT IT CAN BECOME."

- DR. SEUSS. THE LORAX

As America turns out of this dark and discouraging crisis,

and into the bright new dawn of these roaring 20s, we can rejoice in the reality that our country has finally come full circle. America's Perigon has given all Americans, whether Republican, Democrat or Independent, a clean slate and a unique opportunity to set a new course forward. However, far too many of us still do not see the writing on the wall.

Regardless, it is up to those of us who see the big picture to remain steadfast and continue to articulate the truth in the fact that Donald J. Trump is indeed the catalyst for America's Perigon. Fortunately, there are millions of patriots in the enormous movement that he has inspired, who, over the last four years, saw it unfold right before our very eyes. Just as all the proud patriots who supported and followed Lincoln did during the Civil War and America's first Perigon.

Therefore, now the underlying question is:

Will we accept our responsibilities as guardians of our American heritage, and architects of her future, and enlighten our fellow citizens to the truth as they did?

Despite how challenging and precipitous such a task may be, or how tall an order it may seem, we must proceed, and endure that treacherous climb up the mountain together. The peak of that mountain is a place worth reaching. It is where our fellow Americans can achieve what they deserve, that is the opportunity to be enlightened, empowered, and enabled to wake up and accept the truth for themselves.

The more Americans who are awake to that truth, the better,

as this new decade will require all of us to see the bigger picture. Those blind to everything our president and this historic movement are working so vigorously to achieve are missing out. Whether they know it or not, they are living in a false reality devoid of truth.

The truth is that Donald J. Trump is not merely a partisan president, like our founders, Lincoln, JFK, Ronald Reagan, and all of our greats. He is a president fighting for and leading the entire American citizenry, whether you like or dislike him as a person or in the way with which he articulates that leadership. The fact is, he is still our president, and he is going to get the job done regardless.

Like Lincoln himself, President Trump stepped in at the perfect time to bring our country and politics full circle. Now these 2 great disruptors and their brutal honesty were tailor-made for their respective eras. History only bestows such transformative and transcendent leaders when our country is beyond the point of no return. America was nearly there during our American Civil War, and more recently before Trump's improbable but fated victory in 2016.

Since his election, he has given every effort of his body, mind, and soul, to fix our broken country, and bring us back to greatness. Under his leadership, we have seen America operate on cylinders not seen since the days of Presidents John F. Kennedy and Ronald Reagan. Therefore, the choice for Americans in 2020, and every election to come, has never been more apparent.

The Democrat Party and its leaders want to destroy our nation, as they have demonstrated for many years now by inciting hate, division, and intolerance throughout our country. Now, they have taken their evil intentions even further, by encouraging violence, lawlessness, theft, and anarchy throughout our cities. Unfortunately, conservatives, Republicans, and Trump supporters are the ones who they target.

Every day, we see them employing domestic terrorist organizations like "ANTIFA" to do their bidding by burning flags, destroying monuments and churches, looting businesses, and murdering innocent, law-abiding American citizens all over our country. These heartless individuals send a clear message to us all that they are determined to destroy our country, our history, and everything for which we hold dear.

Therefore, the modern Democrat platform is not one in which America, or any nation's people, can place their hopes and dreams, nor give their vote. A vote for the Democrats is a vote for utter chaos and disorder. That is why we, the people, must take the proper steps to ensure this nightmare scenario of chaos ends for good, and save our future from socialism and destruction.

First, we MUST re-elect President Trump for a second term as he will not only restore law and order and protect our history but also finish this historic crusade in which history will remember forever. We need all Americans' collective efforts to work together with our president and fundamentally transition our country to the sort of greatness of those sunny days in the early 1960s. For only a great America is one capable of moving forward and providing its citizens with the promise of a better future.

Secondly, we must recognize that our government, and many of the career politicians it has produced on both sides of the aisle, were running wild in the Washington swamp before Trump triggered America's Perigon. The days of their brand of politics where anything goes, nothing gets done, and everyone gets re-elected regardless, are over. We cannot accept that kind of systemic corruption and must continue draining the murky swamp of all its lingering creatures.

Instead, we must elect leaders who, like Jefferson, Lincoln, Kennedy, Reagan, and Trump, exercise the gold standard of leadership, the brand that transcends Democrat and Republican partisanship, as well as right and left, leading for all the American people.

Two words come to mind, AMERICA FIRST, not if, but, or when, but FIRST.

Ultimately, the task is incumbent on the millennial generation, and those after, to decide what will become of our future. Whether we choose greatness and gain the opportunity to move ourselves and our country forward, hinge on this critical election and how well those of us who understand and comprehend the truth of America's Perigon can muster the courage to articulate it to others. If we can, we will fulfill our duty as heirs of that first revolution.

We can then capitalize on every opportunity to seize the new frontiers of tomorrow and build a better future worthy of our founder's revolutionary promise. But this will only come to pass by combining the best of the old ideas, with brand new ones that equal these incredible times. It will also require us to come together, recognize, and then meet our obligations and responsibilities as citizens of this country, and thus custodians of freedom, liberty, and America's timeless heritage and innate destiny.

When the last greatest generation of Americans was dead set on making their Great America move forward, they rose to the occasion. Although their efforts were inevitably cut short, we have another shot with this new generation. That generation had America's timeless revolutionary spirit and articulated this nation's historical purpose and infinite potential to young Americans with all the potential in the world. We have that chance now, we have that example, and we have everything we will ever need at our disposal.

In this decade of the 20s, it will be required of us all to put aside the differences among us that don't matter, never have, and never will, and leave them in the past where they belong. Only then can we build a future that is both unprecedented and enduring.

Unlike many advanced civilizations, American's have always possessed the innate ability to listen, adapt, endure, and compromise for the greater good, especially when we close our minds off to the noise and look within ourselves. For if nothing else, collectively, the same fire burns deeply within every one of our hearts, and with it, the shared belief that our best and brightest days are just ahead.

But we will need to assess and consider every new idea, solution, invention, and innovation on the journey forward, regardless of how our means and methods may differ.

The fact is that this generation has more tools available than any in our nation's history, to achieve incredible things for this country. Our innate American ability to accomplish the impossible will only benefit from these ever-advancing technological tools at our disposal. However, without our timeless American principles such as individual liberty, personal responsibility, and adherence to basic human morality, none of this is possible. These principles both establish our proper role as masters of new ideas and innovations, and ensure they will be used and not abused, for all Americans.

As Americans, we must recognize the dire need to defend and expand our freedom, so we can secure the promise of even more knowledge and even more significant innovations. Ultimately, it is up to us to share those gifts, and work together to implement them, as we tackle the challenges of tomorrow, and seize the new frontiers of this new decade.

The young people in America today hunger for transparency, authenticity, and results above all else. That is what this new generation of leaders must give them as we forge a new foundation of leadership. With it, a new standard of excellence, one made possible by an America that has come full circle and fully transitioned back to greatness.

We, the American people, are done with the era of controlled and managed decline. This new decade can be an historic decade of creation and forward progress that pivots our nation toward a higher plane of existence and meaning.

The '20s may have started troubled, but together, we can, and we will make them ROAR nonetheless.

CHAPTER 14

Final Thoughts

In the final analysis, my fellow citizens, in this magnificent country of ours, the truth is that we, the people of America, are united in our shared citizenship and the infinite potential it gives us all. More importantly, we are united as fellow human beings and equal brothers and sisters in the eyes of our almighty God.

Therefore, it is high time we endeavor to set our trivial disagreements aside and embrace our roles as equally important pieces of the American puzzle. We must recognize where we are at this point in history, as we peer into the darkness of uncertainty, and illuminate the torch of truth to light the path forward. On this road ahead, like it or not, we must remember that we are all on this journey together, no matter our differences. Those differences and deviations between us are needed just as much as we need one another, for they make us stronger than we can imagine, and will ultimately propel us forward to our destination. Greatness is the aim of every one of us, and service to others is the way to get there.

As Theodore Roosevelt once said, "Each for all, all for each."

Let that be the keystone in the new foundation of leadership that we establish for our children and their children's children. A foundation equal to the one our founding fathers laid, but one that equals the times to which future generations of Americans can draw upon for direction and unlimited strength when we are gone.

We must ensure that they will not have to endure an America that has fallen short of her potential, nor one lacking in her mighty spirit, because that spirit gives all of her citizens the infinite capacity for greatness. We must never forget that.

Nor can we forget that an America made great again, is an America that can move again.

A new generation of American patriots stand ready and more equipped than any in our nation's history to ensure that it happens.

In the words of the great Frank Sinatra, I have "High Hopes" for America's future, and upon the conclusion of this book, I hope that you do too.

Because "The Best is Yet To Come," and we too have a rendezvous with destiny.

See you there.

Driving the Trump Mobile in Harrisburg PA
Photo provided by Vincent Fusca

AFTERWORD

The future of the American people and our great country has always been the responsibility of both our leaders and citizenry to adhere to the very ideals that have preserved our nation for hundreds of years.

America's Perigon should serve not only as a warning in these uncertain times, but as a blueprint for how we are to continue to preserve the United States of America and everything that holds us together as a people.

President's Lincoln, Kennedy, Reagan and Trump have all helped maintain the steady balance between honoring the ideas that made this nation great and cultivating new ideals that allow the United States to remain nimble in this ever-changing world. Most of all, these men know that to forge forward into the future, we must look to the past and use our history as a guiding light to ensure that we do not lose our identity.

To ignore the bond between Lincoln, Kennedy, Reagan and Trump is to ignore the core fabric of freedom that allows the United States of America to continue on the path towards greatness.

We as a people and nation have never shied away from advancement and innovation. As a radical mob threatens to reverse course and send us into a spiral towards socialism, WE THE PEOPLE must stand up and fight back. This is a time for greatness and true progress, not a time for regression.

Bobby Jeffries, the author of America's Perigon, represents the new generation of leadership in American politics. A brand of leadership that is not afraid to think outside of the box while holding true to our founding principles. In this new era, President Trump, like Reagan, Kennedy and Lincoln before him, has inspired people like Jeffries to join the political conversation.

As Roger Stone once said, "He can ride that hair ALL THE WAY to the White House!"

— Jacob Engels
Orlando Florida
July 21, 2020

Photo provided by Jacob Engels

ABOUT THE AUTHOR

Bobby Jeffries is a graduate of Millersville University, former Congressional Candidate, and currently works as a Director of Logistics, Warehousing, and Shipping for a health and wellness company in Harrisburg PA. As a lifelong resident of Hershey, Pennsylvania, Jeffries strives to continue making a positive difference for his community, state, and country by articulating the critical importance of the rigorous defense, and continued preservation of our nation's most timeless founding principles and sacred values. You can follow Bobby's work at BobbyForPA.com and on Twitter, Instagram, and Parler: @BobbyJeffriesPA